CUrtIs DAycArE

Doreen Barnett

Illustrated by: Ronie Pios

ISBN: Softcover   978-1-5144-8066-3
        EBook   978-1-5144-8044-1

Print information available on the last page

Rev. date: 04/18/2016

To order additional copies of this book, contact:
Xlibris
1-888-795-4274
www.Xlibris.com
Orders@Xlibris.com

CUrtIs DAycArE

Doreen Barnett

Illustrated by: Ronie Pios

Today I am going to the day care for the first time. I'm scared. I hope to make friends there.

I took off my Spider-Man pajamas and put on clothes all by myself. I think I'm ready for the babysitter.

My mommy helped me pack my lunch in my favorite Spider-Man bag.

Mommy held my hand on the way to the babysitter. I don't feel scared when I'm with my mommy.

We arrived at Donna's Day Care. The place was big. I held on tight to my mom's hands. My heart was beating fast. My mom rang the bell, and we entered.

I saw a large room with alphabets on the wall. I saw a girl, and she said, "Hello, my name is Denise."

I said, "Hello, my name is Curtis," in a low voice.

Denise seems nice, and she has glasses. Wow.

I went to the next room. There I met two boys. *Yeah!* The first boy's name is Charles. He has a short haircut. The second boy's name is Tony. He has a curly hair. They asked for my name. I said, "Curtis," and I felt happy.

There was another room—the game room. I saw a guitar, drums, a doll house, tic tac toe, and a huge rug in the middle of the room.

I thought, "This is fun. I'm happy here."

My mommy and I went to the backyard. Denise was sliding. Tony and Charles were swinging. I waved to my mommy, letting her know it's ok. I blew my mommy a kiss to tell her bye-bye. My mommy had the biggest smile on her face. My mom now knows I'm not afraid. I have friends.

My friends and I had a good nap. After that, my friends and I ate lunch. This is the coolest part of the day. Denise, Charles, Tony, and I were smiling and laughing while we were eating. We are happy.

At the end of the day, I ran to my mommy and gave her the biggest hug. I told her, "Mommy, I miss you. Mommy, I had fun. Mommy, I have the best friends. Mommy, I can't wait for tomorrow." I was talking nonstop to my mommy, but she was all ears.

She said, "So you see, it wasn't scary after all."

Printed in the United States
By Bookmasters